The Witches Book of Spells

by

Roc Marten

Revised Edition
First Printing 2012
Cover Art by M. Cage

Contents

How Witchcraft and Spells Came to Be

The definition of witchcraft depends on what field of study you are coming from. However, it is synonymous, most often than not, to sorcery, magic, and spell work.

The dictionary defines it as the "art of bringing magical or preternatural power to bear" and the "influence of magic, sorcery, or charms." In science, witchcraft is associated with the use of psychic mechanisms to generate wicked powers without rituals and spells. Meanwhile, Social Anthropology, a study on human social behavior, classifies witchcraft as an ideology that explains various human misfortunes. It involves a supernatural being or a person capable of inflicting harm on an individual or a community in general.

A witch is a practitioner of witchcraft. The origin of the word came from Anglo-Saxon's "wicca," meaning wise. Also related to Middle Low German, "wicken" means "to conjure."

The history of witchcraft is as old as the rich history of human evolution. Some studies say the first witches were healthcare providers who discovered medicinal plants and herbs that affect euphoric emotions. This discovery led to shamanism, where a chemical-induced person talks to divine beings through rituals. Because of their abilities as a medium, they assumed roles significant in social decisions.

The evolution of witchcraft practices came side by side with the evolution of these assumed roles. The pagan beliefs blended with the Indo-European groups and spawned practices such as potions, casting spells, as well as performing works of magic. As religion became superior, witchcraft receded to the periphery of society. This time, it was branded as demon worship.

Primarily, witchcraft practices involve communication with the dead and divine spirits, weather manipulation, many medical applications, as well as influence on human being's mind, body, and will through casting spells. The negative witchcraft is usually called cursing and hexing. The latter—casting of spells—is the most apparent and known ability of a witch. The dictionary defines spell as "a word or formula to have a magical power." Hence, a spell consists of a set of words as well as rituals and actions. Most of the time, it is the combination of words, rituals, and materials.

The power of spells is based on the energy a practitioner puts into the rituals, or sometimes the will of the wisher to put negative or positive effect on an individual.

Spells are cast on varied methods; each has varying requirements, effects, and consequences. Some examples of casting spells are by inscription of rune or sigils on an object to give the object magical powers. Another method involves the immolation or binding of a wax or clay image—usually witches use puppets—to affect an individual. There are also spells that require recitation of incantations, performance of physical rituals, and the use of herbs and medicinal plants.

Varying classifications of spell are known today. For example charms on love and success, spells on love, money, fertility, as well as ways to break curses. You may also encounter terms such as black magic, Voodoo dolls, Rudraksh beads, Hoodoo and so on.

What Are Spells?

In a word, spells mean prayers. For some, it would look like "magic prayers". Prayers, as everyone knows, affect the very fabric of reality itself when uttered and requested.

When there is a tear in this reality, a prayer repairs and restructures that part of the fabric once again, restoring it to its pristine, original self. This is one of the ways the universe renews itself.

With each spell performed, every prayer, each word within every prayer (and even the very letters of the words of every prayer) has a precise meaning aimed for a precise effect. And, thus producing the final result of a successful spell casting.

Divine intervention

When a spell is asked to be performed on your behalf, you are actually asking for a Divine intervention to take place in your situation. It is extremely important for you to understand that spells are not playthings to toy around.

The main point is that you have what the person is doing for you. In requesting a spell on your behalf, you must take the time to understand the type of spells the spell caster will perform.

Through the ages, there are many types of practices that can issue spells. Some of them would include Alchemy, Animism, Bonpo, Druidry, Egyptian Enochian, Hermeticism, Mantrik Hinduism, Hoodoo, Huna, Jewish Witchcraft, Hermetic Kabbalah, Nagualism, Quimbanda, Reiki, Santeria, Shamanism, Voodoo, Wicca, and many more listed around the world.

Protocols

In all of these styles, you have to understand that each requires a particular set of protocols and things you have to give up. The most important would be the rules that you will have to follow.

In some, the spells are accompanied by talismans and charms or amulets in order for these spells to work. This is not actually true for all of them, only on some intense, lower spells.

If these spells (or prayers, if you like) are performed correctly and all the protocols are in place, the request is granted and can have a dramatic impact on the intended person or situation. This happens even if the person is on the other side of the world.

Deity and entities

During the performance of spells, deity and other spiritual entities are invoked to help make a success of these spells or prayers. Since these entities are pure energies themselves, spells are more in directing and guiding them to do things in aid of the spells.

There are other aids in casting spells. Witches use stones, herbs, candles, and others in order to attract the kind of energies needed for the present spell.

Over time, the spell caster builds up rapport with certain entities and deity. Hence, their spells become more effective. When you ask for a spell from a witch, know that every effort is exerted for its success.

Common Myths about Spells

When talking about witchcraft, we usually think about black magic and how it has put humankind into danger, whether it is scenes from the books or from movies. Magic and spell-casting are surrounded by myths and misconceptions that eventually buried its true essence and principles.

What are these myths and how come they are not real?

Myth 1: Those who practice spell-casting and magick worship the Devil or Satan.

For those who practice and follow witchcraft, good and evil is relevant. What is important is that every magic or spell cast is carefully thought over and it would not harm anyone. In addition to that, the Devil or Satan is a Christian construct. It is not included in the witch's pantheon.

Hell is another Christian construct and Wiccans and Pagan followers do not believe in it. It does not mean that because they are not concerned with hell they would commit evil acts. Wiccans and Pagans commit good acts because they know that this would reflect later on in their lives and even in their next life.

Myth 2: Spells have that visual and sound effects just like in Harry Potter films.

Spells, for Wicca followers and Pagan believers, are like prayers for Christians. They can be a way of communicating with the universe your intent or desire. Spells could also be a way of communicating with the gods and goddesses.

Spells do not have the sound and video effects like they are displayed in movies. In fact, spells do not have or manifest within a specific time frame, as Hollywood leads you to believe. Usually, it would take weeks or even months before the spells you cast to take effect.

Myth 3. Casting spells would require very rare materials.

Casting spells do not require you to use rare and weird materials, once again, as the movies would lead you to believe. Spell-casters usually use natural materials such as herbs, incense, candles, oils, flowers and other essences. In spell-casting, what are important is the emotion and the intent. Focusing your energy and using materials to contain and direct your energy towards your intent are the things that would make your spell a success.

Myth 4. Spells backfire.

For Wiccans, every spell or action must be carried out as long as it does not cause any harm to others. They call this rule, "The Wiccan Rede." Aside from that, Wiccans and Pagan followers strongly believe in the Law of Threefold. Whatever is done would return back in threefold. In this sense, it does not mean that spells backfire, it would just show that whatever is done will come back to you. Good intentions and positive wishes would not create negative effects.

Myth 5. Spells can make things possible out of thin air.

Spells turn possibilities into reality. They cannot make things happen out of nowhere. A love spell cannot make a superstar singer fall in love with you and sing you love songs if you have not even met him or her once. A love spell will not turn a beast into a prince charming.

Spells – Features and Characteristics

Like any endeavor, casting spells takes on different forms and styles, the number of which depends on the number of the casters themselves. Spells have specific formulas that must be recited or performed by the spell caster.

These spells are usually constructed from words, gestures, and ingredients. When a spell involves words, these words must be pronounced clearly, firmly, and emphatically. They cannot be whispered, but said in a conversational level.

Where gestures are needed, the gesture will require freedom of movement of arms, hands and fingers. Some specifically require further movements, sometimes.

The spells that require ingredients usually mean the destruction of these material ingredients. Most often, these ingredients used for any spell can only be used once.

The most common ingredients include hand-made or personalized candles for burning, incense, essential oils, silk cloths, some specific metals, special herbs, specific gemstones, crystals, and some powders.

Reverse spells

Some spells are cast in two forms – a normal form, and its reverse. Light may be cast in the form of Darkness. The reversed form usually requires different ingredients from the normal form.

Duration

Spells have durations, and are called "concentrations". These are the spells that remain in force for as long as the caster maintains concentration on it. Most, however, have a limited duration that varies according the level of the spell itself. The spell caster does not have to concentrate to keep these spells in effect.

Depending on the gravity of the request, the rituals for spell casting can take a day, three days, a week or even longer. Some are done only at night, sometimes only at sunrise, and some only on a specific day or week or month.

Some can be performed only during the waning or waxing of the moon depending on the requirements.

Once the spell is cast, it will last according to its intended duration, and the spell caster can move on to other tasks. The caster can end any spell with a non-permanent duration.

Some spells, once cast, act immediately, and are done. Other spells are permanent. After the immediate action of the magic, the non-magical effects remain enforced.

Personal spells

Many spells are unique in the sense that they are known only by a single order or by the individual caster. The coven or the individual caster is expected to guard their personal spells.

Personal spells known only to the caster might be given to the coven that the caster belongs to. It might also be kept private until the caster's death when the coven takes hold of the caster's spell books.

Those spell casters who die without any guild or coven they belong to might have their original spells lost for years until somebody recovers their spell books.

Why Magic Spells May Not Work

There are different kinds of spells that can be used to achieve different kinds of goals. It could be about wealth, health, and the most famous, love. There may be people who would testify with the effectiveness of the spells, while there are others who may say that they are not getting anything out of them.

But why do spells fail? Followers and experts would say there are many contributing factors why spells do not work.

Reason 1:
Spell-casting is all about directing your spiritual energies towards one goal. A clouded mind would result into an energy that can prevent what you desire from happening. In short, your mind should be in sync with the kind of spell you are going to use. The practitioner should believe in the spell for it to manifest.

Discipline is important. Concentration and focus is crucial when sending and making your intent one with the universe and its energy. This focus and concentration may be difficult to achieve immediately. Getting an experienced mentor could help you develop this kind of trait.

Reason 2:
Spell-casters would say that one of the major reasons why spells do not work is experience. The internet is a rich source of spells that are written by experienced spell-casters and those who only claim success. When following spells on the internet, you could always ask the caster for any proof that they have succeeded with their spells.

The experience of the person who is casting the spell is also crucial. Casting spells is not just about reading the incantation; it is also about studying the occult or the system.

Reason 3:
Of course, you would not get anywhere if you are using the wrong spells and the wrong materials. There are spells which may not work for a person but may work for other people. You can keep track of the spells that are not working for you. Although, you could also consider that they may not be working because you may lack concentration and focus while casting the spell. You could also write your own spell, especially if you cannot find anything that would suit your personality and your particular situation. Writing spells is not easy. Again, it would require studies and patience.

Reason 4:
Strong belief and patience are important. If you miss this, then you would surely think that the spell is bound to fail. A spell-caster should believe in his or her spell, if not, then who else would believe that it will work.

Spell-casters need to be patient. Spells do not work over night. There are times the results of a spell for a very long period of time. If a spell-caster would cast a spell and expect it to happen within a year and nothing happened after a year, then it could mean that the spell is not meant to work for that period of time. The objective or the goal could manifest into your life after a year or even longer. Sometimes, it would even surpass what you expect.

Reason 5:
Another reason why spells did not work can be because of the negativity surrounding the caster. It could be real or imagined, but negative energy could definitely affect the spell. A caster should remove any negative thinking when casting spells. Aside from that, most casters would prefer performing spells in private to avoid public scrutiny and at the same time, avoid negative energy.

Spells, Hexes and Vibrations

Attested to by even the most primitive of tribes since ancient times, the power of the spoken word was never questioned ever. These powerful spoken words are now called spells, hexes, curses and vibrations.

The power of the word is further amplified if the spell-giver is known to be well-versed in his conjuring craft. Adding terror to the spell is the use of alien words from an unheard-of language known only to the magic man.

Making a spell or a curse with dramatic displays of strange words and smoke and potions or even by a simple use of the hand was prevalent ever since the medieval times. The intended person under a curse was believed to be totally powerless over his fate.

Spells

Developed over the centuries by ancient priests and shamans, the spells created became established formulas. Because they were proven to be effective, they were written down for future use.

In Egypt, the prescriptions in using these spells became more detailed. Aside from having them written down, there were specific directions on how to use voice and all other exacting accoutrements related to spell-giving.

Those in the know in the occult arts readily concede that the power of a spell stays enforced until such time when that spell's energy is neutralized. Also contributing to the spell's effectiveness is in the maker's strong belief.

The famous voodoo in the Caribbean involves hexing, cursing and projecting spells. The spells are phrased from an established format, including the rituals, and delivered with strong emotions and body movements by the witch doctor.

Hexes

Just like spells, hexes are powerful negative thoughts expressed in strong emotional outbursts from the hex-giver. It is said that the more energy expended in the hexing ritual, the more effective it will be.

From the receiver, it is the fearful emotions in the subconscious mind that helps convince the victim of the effectiveness of the hex.

A curse or a hex could not affect anybody unless there were still people who are using an energetic band that influence other people. If a spell given out 100 years or more ago, and there was nobody to fuel it with energy, that hex would have been dissolved and would no longer exist in our present energy fields.

Vibrations

If a spell or a curse is discovered today, then there is a group that actively uses that kind of energy. Whatever negative energies these are – hate, pain, hurt, or suffering – the group is using the vibrations to create a vortex to attract that kind of energy into their circle.

These groups commonly use a circle to amplify their desired energy. In the circle would be objects (pentagrams, triangles, snakes, bones, etc.) to attract and hold the desired vibrations. They perform ceremonies using this energy for whatever purpose they have in mind.

The circles are set up on the earth's natural grid, amplifying their energies. These groups have knowledge on the power of these grids, and they know how to run them and project energy.

So far, these kinds of spells have not been detected of late. Either the groups responsible for them are inactive or that they might have disbanded for the time being.

What is White Magic and Black Magic

White Magic

The first point I would like to point out is that white magic is not of any particular tradition. White magic is more a general philosophy of magic than anything else. The philosophy of white magic is simply this: magic is to heal and to help, not to harm and to create hardships.

Regardless of what the ritual looks like and what it can do, every spell is part of white magic if it does no harm to anyone or anything. A love spell therefore falls under white magic because of the simple reason that it helps two people fall happily in love.

Black Magic

Black magic is the practice of magic that draws on assumed malevolent powers. This type of magic is invoked when attempting to perform a spell that is evil in nature, such as wishing to kill, steal, injure, cause misfortune or destruction, or for personal gain without regard to harmful consequences. As a term, "black magic" is normally used by those that do not approve of its uses, commonly in a ritualistic setting; the argument of "magic having no color, and it is merely the application and use by its user," backs the claim that not everything termed as "black magic" has malevolent intentions behind it, and some would consider it to have beneficial and benevolent uses.

A different view on Black Magic is used in Chaos Magick. In this branch of practice, spells sometimes correspond to colors, depending on the supposed effect. Black Magic, according to Chaos Magick, corresponds to magic that is performed around the themes of death, separation, severance and entropy.

In the end, White magic is used to heal, not harm.

Black magic is used to cause harm and generally intended for evil purposes.

Black magic is used to cause harm and generally intended for evil purposes.

Spells and The Moon

Spells work best in tandem with nature's mysterious, magical and powerful objects. Of these, the moon is number one on the list for spell-casters.

The following are some refresher notes on spells and the phases of the moon.

New Moon / Dark Moon

Just like the full moon, the new moon (or dark moon) is the most opportune time to remove things from our lives. It is usually the time when you are most powerful in spell-giving.

This is a good time to reverse spells others have cast, ideal for banishing spells and focusing on the replacement of any negative effects all around.

However, keep in mind that when asking for something to be removed, there is a void left open. Ask for something positive and fill up that space.

To prevent a waxing influence on your spell work, the banishing spells and rituals must be done before the beginning of the new moon. The most powerful time for spells is three days after the appearance of the new moon.

Black Moon

When two new moons appear during a single month, the second new moon is regarded as the stronger of the two. This is the best time to cast spells that deal on addiction.

Waxing Moon

The time of the waxing moon to full moon is the best time to cast spells on situations and events that concerns us. The waxing moon is perfect for spell work regarding success, protection, abundance, friendships, luck, new beginnings, and love.

The waxing moon is wonderful for good, constructive magic.

First Quarter

This is the mid-point between the new moon and the full moon. This is the time most ideal in focusing and meditating on attracting new positive things toward you. These things will grow as the moon waxes.

Waxing gibbous

This is the perfect time to focus on fruition and completion of your spell work, and the time to focus and meditate on all the spell work you did during the waxing phase.

This is also good to do any magical work on prophecy, protection or divination.

Full Moon

This is the time to meditate on the divine power of the universe and pray that it shall also strengthen and empower us. The full moon imparts the strongest power for all invocations and spells.

This is the time to cast your most powerful magic spells. To avoid a waning influence, cast your spells and do your rituals before the exact time of a full moon.

Blue Moon

When a month has two full moons, the 2nd full moon is deemed the stronger and more powerful. For your spells and rituals that need an extra kick, this is the time to do them.

This is also the time to meditate on your life's goals and to assess your successes and failures.

Waning Gibbous

This is the best time to banish the things we don't want anymore in our lives. Plus, it is time to meditate on cleansing and removing all negativity around us.

Last Quarter

This is the time for ending things, much like the moon going to the end of its cycle. Focus and meditate on balancing your body's energies, replacing negatives with positives.

Waning Moon

The time of the waning to the new moon is also the best time to remove unwanted circumstances in our lives. Cast banishing spells against enemies, addictions, sickness, negativity, and evil. Cleanse yourself of the things you no longer need.

Preparing For A Spell

Casting spells is not just about reading incantations and using candles and incense. There are more to it than reading lines and waiting for the outcome. For some, especially Wiccans, using or casting spells is a part of their religious belief. Casting spells is considered to be an intentional use of the universe's power that already exists around us.

Casting or using spells would require meditation and directing the spell-caster's spiritual energy into the desired outcome. Directing your personal energy means that a person should have an understanding of the power "within" the person. For example, casting a spell may require some items like candles, etc. The spell-caster should evoke imagery and visualize the goal while holding the items. This practice would direct the energy towards the items that would help in achieving the goals.

There are strict guidelines that should be followed when casting or using spells. Wiccans would follow the "The Wiccan Rede" which states that "do what ye will, harm ye none." This clearly states that Wiccans could perform rituals and spells but its effect or consequences should be recognized first. For harm done to others and nature, "will return three-fold." Spell-casting cannot be used for anger, revenge, and jealousy.

Aside from being clear with your intentions, you should also be clear in what situation you will be using the spell. There are different kinds of spells, all depending on the situation. There are healing, love, energy, wealth, peace and other kinds of spells.

There are spells that can be modified to suit the needs and situation of the spell-caster. There are some spells which would require the spell-caster to use the exact words, while some would say that those spells which are spoken by the spell-caster's own words are more pure and powerful.

Spell-casting would also use different tools or methods. These tools would contain the energy that can be used to represent your desires and goals. There are different kinds of tools like oils, candles, cards, stones, runes, etc. Most of the times, the object used is something associated with the objective or intent. For example, if it is a money spell, loose change can be used as a tool.

The location where to cast the spell is also important. Wiccans believe that we are in one with nature. They may have some rituals and practices that would require them to be with nature, however, spell-casting can also be done privately. Some Wiccan followers would often conduct their practices secretly, not only to avoid public persecution but to contain their energies and direct them towards their goal.

When casting a spell, it is important to keep it mind that we are using our energy and directing it to achieve a desired outcome. The universe is full of energy. Therefore, there could be negative energy that could interfere with how we use ours. Performing privately would ensure that our energy and our spell are not disturbed.

Another common problem among spell-casters is the timing. Some spells would require specific time to perform them. Adapting to time phase could be hard. There are some expert spell-catchers whom would say that performing spells under a full moon, for instance, is not that important. It can increase the potency of the spell, but it is the intention that is more important. Directing our mind and spiritual energy towards our objective would be the determining factor on how effective our spells would be.

** A Special Note**
Within this spell collection you will find spells that fall into the realm of white magic and others that fall into the realm of black magic. You have a choice as to which type of magic you perform. It is not my place to tell you which type of magic to perform nor do I want to. You have to decide for yourself.

Love Spells

Love is the most powerful human emotion. Love has the power to make you or break you. Love spells are often seen as manipulative and in most cases are carried out to control a love relationship. Love spells can be carried out with both positive and negative energy. Spells containing positive energy are likely to strengthen a relation and improve the relationship while spells containing negative energy can produce dire consequences for the spell-caster. If you're planning to perform a love spell always keep in mind that you cannot win someone's love through manipulation. Performing a love spell in such a way is unethical and could have negative results.

Love Spell #1- To Hear From Your Lover
Items needed to perform this spell: A red candle and a crystal

It is best to perform this spell when the moon is waxing. Take a photo of your lover and a photo of yourself. Using a paper clip, hook the photos together so that the faces are on top of each other.

Recite the following:
I call on forces higher then I,
To awaken the dreams that I hold inside,
Through this connection that knows my need,
I ask for love's enchantment with all speed.
May this work for me in the most correct way attracting the love I need today....
I call on thee in perfect love & trust working with me sending what's just...
Harming none and helping all is how it shall be
This I make true 3x3x3.

Take the photos and place them at the bottom of your underwear drawer. The person should soon write, call, or reappear.

Love Spell #2 – To Find a Mate

Items needed to perform this spell: A small sample of your favorite scent or fragrance, 1 pink candle and a crystal.

Carve a heart in your candle with a toothpick or something similar. Light the candle in a window where it will receive moonlight (full moon light is best). Put the
scent container in front of the candle and say:

Venus, grant me the love that I lack;
Through this scent, my mate attracts!

Let the candle burn out naturally, then carry the scent with you, spraying on a small amount whenever you are out or may be meeting people. Increase the power of the
magic by repeating the invocation as you put on the scent!

Love Spell #3 – To Obtain the Love of a Specific Person

Items needed to perform this spell: Cauldron or something similar to contain a fire, 3 inch by 3 inch piece of paper, 1 Red Crayon or Marker.

During the nighttime hours light a small fire in a cauldron. Cut out a piece of paper that is 3 inches by 3 inches. Draw a heart on the paper and color it in with red. Write the name of the name of the person that you desire on the heart. While doing this think of this person being attracted to you. Think of his or her heart burning with desire for you just like the flames of the fire. Then kiss the name on the heart 3 times. Place the paper in the fire while saying these words 3 times. Do so with sincerity...

Fire come from below,
bring me love that I do know,
make my heart blaze and shine,
to bring the love that will be mine!
Soon my love will come a day,
three times strong and here to stay!

SO MOTE IT BE!

Meditate on the spell you just did, visualizing it to come true! After you are Done meditating, extinguish the fire. Soon your love will come to you!

Love Spell #4 – Bring Back My Lover

Items needed to perform this spell: Two white candles, a photo of your lover, a photo of yourself smiling, a chamomile tea bag, and a piece of blue cloth.

This ritual should be performed at 8:00 pm. Light the candles and relax yourself by taking several deep breaths. Imagine a very peaceful scene, somewhere beautiful. Once relaxed, hold the picture of your ex-lover in your hand and repeat the following...

"With the light of the flame I'll light your desire,
When I speak your name you'll feel my fire,
The spell has been cast So Be It!"

Repeat your ex-lovers name 3 times, slowly. Place your picture on top of his, face to face. Wrap the two pictures along with the tea bag in the blue cloth. Put the package in a safe place. For the next three weeks, light the candles at 8:00 each night and say your ex-lovers name three times.

Love Spell #5 – To Attract A Lover (A Norse Spell)

Items needed to perform this spell: 1 Pink Candle, 1 Pink Crystal

Mark the candle and the crystal with the Ing, Gyfu and Bjork Runes. Light the candle and place the crystal beside the candle. Now repeat the following phrase three times:

Three ladies came across the land,
Bringing love into my hand:
The first called him (or her)

The second brought him
The third bound us together

The crystal is then charged to add to the spell. When the candle is finished burning, the
crystal is secreted among personal belongings.

Love Spell #6 – To Maintain Unconditional Love

Items needed to perform this spell: 1 Pink Candle, 1 White Candle, 1 Black Candle, and Incense.

Perform this spell every full moon. Look at the Moon, then light the candles and say:

"The kind Fates have blessed my home,
the kind Fates have blessed my heart,
the kind Fates have blessed my loved ones,
I offer thanks with a humble heart
I thank the Goddess for my life

I thank the Goddess for my love
I thank the Goddess for continued blessings
already on their way.
Blessed be!"

Love Spell #7 – Release an Unwanted Love

Items needed to perform this spell: Athame, 2 Black Candles, 1 Candle of any color to represent the person you are trying to release, 3 candle holders.

This spell is best performed during a wanning moon. Cast a circle for devoking and call upon all corners. Place the two black candles in candle holders and light them. With the candle representing the unwanted love in your left hand and the Athame in your right hand raise your arms above your head and say the following...

Goddess of the Moon, Mother of all, Creator of life,
I ask of thee to bless this candle in the name of _____ .

Place the single candle in a candle holder and light it. Then say the following:

God of the Sun, Horned Consort of the Goddess, Ruler of the Day,
I ask thee to bless this candle in the name of _____ .

Lift the single candle while still in the candle holder above your head and call out the following:

With this candle blessed in the name of_____ .
I command that he does not see me with eyes of love,
but now with the eyes of friends.
In Goddess name I ask. Blessed Be! "

Thank the corners, close your circle, blow out the black candles and allow the single candle to burn out.

Love Spell #8 – Let a Lover Go

Items needed to perform this spell: A picture of you and your ex-lover together, Athame.

Cast your circle and place the picture of you and your ex-lover on your alter. Without thoughts of recrimination or revenge, take your Athame and cut your ex-lover out of the picture. Place the picture of him in the fire and think of a joyful life without this person. Bury the ashes.

Love Spell #9 – Fertility Spell (A spell to get you pregnant)

Items needed to perform this spell: 2 White Candles, Incense

Light both candles along with the incense and say the following:

"I beg of you Goddess hear my plea, fulfill my wish and fulfill my need, bear new life into my womb, so happiness can adorn my home, as I will so mote it be, with no harm come back to me..."

Repeat this spell as many times as you deem necessary. When you are done blow out the candles, but allow the incense to burn and let the spell leave with the smoke.

Love Spell #10 – Loving Marriage Spell

Items needed to perform this spell: 1/2 cup of rock salt , 1/2 cup of coconut oil, 1/2 cup of white rice, 2 handfuls of gardenia petals(or similar white flower), 5 drops of ylang ylang oil

Mix together all ingredients during a full moon. Save the mixture in a cool location until your wedding night. On your wedding night, you and your partner should bath together with the ingredients you mixed together dispersed in your bath water. This spell will ensure a happy start to your marriage.

Love Spell #11 – Make Your Marriage Last Forever
Items needed to perform this spell: Red rose petals, Rose water, Lavender, Jasmine scented candle, Black Ink Pen or Marker.

This spell should be performed before going to bed. Remove the petals of the rose from the flower. Write the name of your spouse and yourself on the rose petals with your black ink pen or marker. Dip the petals in rose water and place the petals under your bed cover. Light the Jasmine scented candle. Turn out the lights and repeat the following two times..

Oh Venus, the Goddess of love
It is my humble prayer to thee
That my marriage, the both of us
Forever we may be.

Depending on the current status of your relationship this spell can be performed once or twice per month.

Financial Luck Spells

Financial luck spells are spells focused around wealth and money. The outcome of these raises can appear from many different fronts such as gaining more money from a pay raise at work, finding money on the street and so on. Money spells can also be used to spend your money more wisely and even help you to save money.

Financial Luck Spell #1 – Attract Money
Items needed to perform this spell: 1 Green candle, 1 white candle, anointing oil

This spell should be performed the same time each day or night.
The Green candle represents the money while the white candle represents you. Make sure you anoint the candles with oil first, thinking of your desire for money to come to you. Set the candles on your alter 9 inches apart. After doing so say the following:

"Money, money come to me in abundance three times three
May I be enriched in the best of ways harming none on its way
This I accept, so mote it be bring me money three times three!"
Repeat this for nine days. Each day move the white candle one inch closer to the green candle. When the candles touch, your spell is finished. Make sure you visualize the money pouring in from the universe.

Financial Luck Spell #2 – Money Tree Spell

Items needed to perform this spell: 1 ivy cutting, 1 flowerpot, soil, 1 small lapis lazuli crystal, 1 green candle, 1 candle holder, small watering can.

After planting the ivy cutting in your flower pot, gently place the lapiz lazuli crystal on the soil, not touching the stem of the plant. Place your plant indoors where it will get adequate sunlight and water as necessary. At night place your plant on windowsill where it will receive the Moon's rays. Place the green candle in front of you on a table and light it. Say the following:

Elements gather one by one
Money tree turn to the Sun
Rays of light make my plant grow
Lunar light adds depths and power
With this comes true wealth for me
Enchanted riches to be mine
Yes I say this is to be
Money money come to me

Allow the green candle to burn down completely. Nurture your plant on a daily basis, always gaze at your plant when reciting this spell.

Financial Luck Spell #3 – Conduring Cash
Items needed to perform this spell: 1 green candle. Small green bag or purse. Your wand. Several grains of rice on a dish. 1 Coin. Your stone.

This spell is best done during a waxing moon.

Light your green candle and place your coin in the center of the dish of rice and say the following chant three times:

Sky above and earth below,
See my money grow and grow.

Tap the coin with your wand. Quietly focus on the money coming to you in normal ways. When you are done focusing on the money coming to you place the coin in the small green bag with most of the rice. Leave about 1/6th of the rice to scatter outside. Keep the bag under your pillow when you go to sleep and keep it with your stone in throughout the day.

Repeat the chant once a day until your money comes. When your money does come to you then scatter the rice outside or bury it.

Financial Luck Spell #4 – Money Gaining Spell

Items needed to perform this spell: 1 Silver coin. Cauldron

This spell is best performed during the Full Moon. Fill your cauldron half-full of water and drop a silver coin into it. Position the cauldron so that the light of the Moon shines into the water. Sweep your hands just above the surface of the water, symbolically gathering the Moon's silver.

While doing this, say the following:

Lovely Lady of the Moon, bring to me your wealth right soon. Fill my hands with silver and gold. All you give, my hands can hold.

Repeat the chant three times. When finished, pour the water upon the Earth.

Financial Luck Spell #5 – Money Talisman

Items needed to perform this spell: 5 pumpkinseeds. 3 Cinnamon sticks. One dollar bill. Green cloth. Green candle. Basil oil. Green ribbon

On a Friday during the waxing moon, assemble all your ingredients at dusk. Take the candle and rub (Prosperity, basil or cinnamon) oil into it while focusing on your bills and debts being paid, see them being paid, picture yourself writing checks and smiling all the way to the bank. Light the candle and take the green cloth, add the pumpkinseeds, Cinnamon sticks, and the dollar bill and fold three times, tie with ribbon. Chant the following while you work and focus on money coming towards you;

 "Dollar bill, work your will. Pumpkinseeds do your deeds. Cinnamon sticks, do the trick, Bring needed money & bring it quick".

Repeat the chant three times. Burn the candle for nine minutes. Keep Talisman near your wallet or purse, and bills to be paid. Expect money to come, know it will and it shall.

31

Financial Luck Spell #6 – Powerful Money Spell

Items needed to perform this spell: 1 Green candle. 1 White candle. 1 red candle. 1 Blue candle. 1 Gold candle. A piece of your hair. 1 cloth bag.

Place all four candles in a circle on your alter and light them. Place the white at the top, and the other colors anywhere. Take your hair and your cloth bag put it in the middle.

Pick your hair up and stare into the green candle and say:

With this one strand of hair,
I will get wealthy because it's fair,
I invoke the spirits and want to say,
I need money, O I need it today.

The next time you say it, stare at the white candle, then the blue, then the red, then the gold.

After you're done with the chant, take the bag and put the strand of hair in it. Then finish off the spell by saying:

I will be wealthy,
I will be healthy,
With this strand of hair,
I will get my money,
And it will be fair.

Carry the strand of hair with you always.

Financial Luck Spell #7 – Money or Job Spell

Items needed to perform this spell: 4 tiger's eye crystals. 12 silver coins. 1 piece of paper. Green or brown pen or marker.

Place the four tiger's eye crystals in a square formation leaving room for the silver coins to go between them. Place 4 silver coins between each tiger's eye, creating a square. While you are doing this, picture yourself in that new job, or what you would do with that money.
Write on the piece of paper the job you are seeking, or the amount of money you need, fold the paper up and place it in the center of the square. Trace the square of

tiger's eyes, starting in the East. As you trace it, see yourself doing the job you are seeking, or doing what you want to do with the money you have.

Say at each stone:

Eastern beings see my request,
Bring to me what You think is best.

Northern beings hear my cry,
Bring this opportunity by.

Western beings know what I need,
And let me be the one to succeed.

Southern beings let good fortune come,
So I may have the proper sum.

Perform the chant once a day until you receive what you require.

Financial Luck Spell #8 – Money Pay Back Spell
Items needed to perform this spell: Nothing more than a belief in the spell itself.

Repeat this chant as often as you'd like.

say this chant as many times as you please

You owe what you owe
You reap what you have sown
Just pay it all up enough is enough
I have given you time plenty of time
I just want what is rightfully mine

Financial Luck Spell #9 – Fortune Spinner Spell
Items needed to perform this spell: Any Pendulum, Paper, and Pen

Draw an arced arrow on the top right hand of the paper, label it 'YES', draw a second arced arrow on the bottom right hand side of the paper, label this one 'NO'. Draw a line straight through from left to right, label it 'MAYBE'.
Holding the pendulum above the paper, allow the pendulum rest in the center of the circle. The diagram should make a circle with two arrows pointing at each other.
Ask a 'YES/NO' question about the past present or future. Now let the pendulum swing back and forth, it will start to swing in the direction of the answer: yes, no, or maybe.

Financial Luck Spell #10 – Your Lucky Charm Spell
Items needed to perform this spell: A coin minted on the year you were born.

Empower the coin by repeating the following chant:

By word, will, and this silver coin,
Magick and fortune herin join!

Carry the coin with you at all times.

Healing Spells

The power that accompanies healing spells can be considered the greatest of all spells. In essence, these spells deal with life and death. The healing spells presented in this book can help with a number of ailments, including healing wounds and scars and so on. Caution should always be taken when dealing with health spells. The slightest mishap could produce horrible results.

Healing Spells #1 – Healing a Sunburn Spell
Items needed to perform this spell: Aloe. 1 Red Candle. 1 Candle that closely matches the color of your skin.

Light the red candle and allow it to sit there burning while you perform the spell. Rub the Aloe where the sunburn is while saying the following chant:

The sun has hurt me today.
Its powerful light has inflicted pain on me.
Let it be, the sun has hurt me today.
But this pain shall not stay, for my power is stronger.
So let this wound heal today.

Put out the red candle with water and light the candle that is the color of your skin.

Healing Spells #2 – Cold and Flu Charm
Items needed to perform this spell: Eucalyptus. Anointing oil. 1 blue chord long enough to wrap around your wrist or ankle three times.

Tie a knot in the cord, dab it with anointing oil and say the following:
"Cold be gone, body be strong"

Tie another knot further along the cord, dab with anointing oil and say,

"Cold be gone, body be strong"

Repeat the above step three more times and then tie the cord around your wrist or ankle as you say, *"So Mote It Be"*

Wear the cord for 24 hours and your symptoms should go away.

Healing Spells #3 – Healing Charm
Items needed to perform this spell: Water, Lambs Wool, Silver Knife, Bowl, Scented Oil, Red Wine, White Velvet cloth.

Pour a quart of water into a large bowl, by candlelight, then take a silver knife and write with its point upon the water's surface the name of the illness that afflicts you. Next, soak, a small lock of lamb's wool first in a scented oil and second in some red wine. Carry it to the bowl and drop it in the water, saying the following chant:

The dark be lightened
The harsh be softened
The rank be sweetened
By the power of the blade
And by the power of the water

After saying the chant, leave the lamb's wool there allowing it to soak all night, until sunrise, when it should be removed, wrung out and set to dry upon a small circle of white velvet cloth. The contents of the bowl should be emptied into a hole dug into the earth, and the hole filled again, using the same soil you dug up. When the lamb's wool is dry, it should be sewn up in the velvet and pinned beneath your clothing. Where it for a full month.

Healing Spells #4 – Eliminating Stress
Items needed to perform this spell: A handmade cloth bag (this bag must be hand stitched by you). Dry soil taken from the earth. Borage flowers.

Place the borage flowers along with the soil taken from the earth in your bag. Pull the drawstrings of the bag to secure them. Keep the bag in an easily accessible place. During times of stress place your hands in the bag, touch the dried borage flowers, reflect on your stored memories, and let Mother Earth work her magic.

Healing Spells #5 – Simple Healing Spell
Items needed to perform this spell: 1 Glass of Water

Blow on the water while imagining a circle of light around it. Picture all the pain disappearing.

Say the following:

With this water,
No more pain,
Let it flow away like the sudden rain

Blow again.
Drink the water.

Healing Spells #6 – Heal Physical Pain
Items needed to perform this spell: A piece of amethyst

Take the amethyst and hold it in the hand that is closest to the pain you are feeling. Imagine a comforting light collecting at your feet and draw the light up slowly towards your head filling every part of the body.

While doing this silently say the following chant:

Bright light, shining light
Heal my hurts with all thy might.

Repeat this as you move the light up through your body. Extend the light about a foot beyond your body. Pull the light in and focus the light towards the part of your body in which you are experiencing pain.

Repeat the spell until you feel comfort in the area in which you are in pain. To end the spell
Say the following chant:

Bright light, shining light
Heal my hurts with all thy might.

So mote it be

Healing Spells #7 – Cold Fighting Spell

Items needed to perform this spell: None

In a powerful voice say the following:

Colds, I hate
Colds are bad fate
Colds be gone go go go flee flee flee you don't bring happiness to me!
Go go flee
So mote it be

Healing Spells #8 – Headache Chant

Items needed to perform this spell: None

Concentrate all your thoughts on where the pain is and chant the following three times:

Tame thou flesh and blood, as my sire tames the lion.

Healing Spells #9 – To Stop One from Bleeding

Items needed to perform this spell: None

Say the following while the person is bleeding and you are hovering over:

Red rivers flow as they should, _____ wound has begun to flood. Wind, water, fire and mud, stop _____ river of flowing blood.

Healing Spells #10 – Cure a Sore Throat Spell

Items needed to perform this spell: 1 Cup of Lemon Tea

Perform this spell while holding your hand over the cup of lemon tea and recite the following:

My throat is dry,
My voice is horse,
May this tea break the curse,

Let it flow upon its course,
May my voice be like a bell,
May this tea make me well.

Then drink the tea.

Confidence Spells

Confidence spells are used exactly for what they are named after, building confidence. If you are in need of a confidence boost then these spells will help you achieve the desired results. As with any spells performed, confidence spells do come with a price. Confidence spells must be cast exactly as described for any mistakes in the casting of these spells can have dire consequences on what little confidence you may already have.

Confidence Spells #1 – Increasing Confidence
Items needed to perform this spell: Purple Candles. Rose Essential Oil. Ylang Ylang Essential Oil. Rose Quartz or Amethyst Crystal. Mirror

In your bathroom, light as many purple candles as you would like. The intent here is for the candles to cast light upon the bath water that you will draw. Run your bath water, after turning off the water add five drops of essential oil and five drops of ylang-ylang. Drop both the rose oil and the ylang-ylang into the pools of light. Place a rose quartz or amethyst crystal in the water to strengthen self-love and approval. Lie in the water and swirl the light pools in turn, making an affirmation for each one, for example:

Continue to swirl the light, visualizing it flowing within you, making you a body of light and loveliness. Make a wish for yourself in each light pool.

When you are done with your bath, wrap yourself in a soft towel and let the water drain, while saying:

Doubts and sorrow, flow from me, what I wish, I can be.
Look at yourself in the mirror framed by light and you will see how your inner radiance creates true beauty that cannot fade.

40

Confidence Spells #2 – Self Confidence Spell
Items needed to perform this spell: 1 red candle. Success incense.

Every morning, while standing in front of a mirror. Light the red candle and concentrate on the flame for 30 seconds, then look into your own eyes and say the following:

You are beautiful and can succeed in what you wish

Take a minute or two to visualize yourself happy and fulfilled. Burn the incense as you get dressed.

Confidence Spells #3 – Courage Enchantment Spell
Items needed to perform this spell: A piece of your own jewelry.

Cast a circle and then purify it. Transfer energy into the jewelry you have chosen to use for this spell. While charging the jewelry chant the following:

The meek are weak give me strength courage boundless courage to do things I wouldn't normally do no matter what it is.

Wear the charge jewelry.

Confidence Spells #4 – A Calming Confidence Spell
Items needed to perform this spell: Nothing

Lay, sit or stand in a comfortable position. Close your eyes and take several slow deep breathes feeling your chest rising and falling. Feel the energy building in your chest.
Harness this energy and spread it throughout your body. While taking your deep calming breaths say the following chant:

Lord above
Grant me wit beyond measure
Power to treasure
Bucket loads of confidence
Protection that will never brake
And love to cherish forever more
So mote it be

41

When you are done with the chant and you feel a sense of power flowing through out your body you can open your eyes and stop chanting.

Confidence Spells #5 – Empower and Ascend Spell
Items needed to perform this spell: Nothing

Say the following chant 3 times:

Power to ascend
Please descend unto me
Pass on your knowledge
Oh Great Goddess
Tell your child what
He/She needs to know
As He/She's been feeling rather low
Power from above
I invoke thee
I welcome thee into my body
We must be whole and complete
As one I do your bidding
As one I am your child
Grant me your knowledge
Grant me your power
Be one with me
So mote it be
So mote it be

Hair Spells

Did you know that there are spells for just about anything you could possibly think of? If you can think it, there is probably a spell for it. Including spells that involve your hair. From preventing baldness to growing a head of beautiful hair, there is a spell for it.

Hair Spells #1 – Prevent Hair Loss

Items needed to perform this spell: 1 orange candle. 1 lump of clay. Water to moisten the clay and your head.

Place the water in a container and light the candle. While dripping the candle wax into the water say the following:

Bless this water, make it magic,
Without luck, it will be tragic.
Magic wax and Flame a burning,
Spirits of the World start turning.

Take the clay and roll it out into a flat sheet. Moisten your head with the water and then wrap your head with the clay. Massage the clay softly so you are also massaging your head and say the following:

Magic clay from magic water,
Protect my head from forces wander.
With my fingers in this motion,
Guard my hair and save my fortune.

Repeat the chant several times. When you are finished with this spell, wash the clay off of your head and hair.

Hair Spells #2 – To Make Your Hair Grow

Items needed to perform this spell: 1 candle (any color). A cloth. Dirt. Water.

Light the candle and allow the wax to drip into the water while saying the following:

Colored wax infest this water,
And from the flame make it grow hotter,
And from the mixture soon to be,
Grow some hair for all to see.

Then mix in the dirt while chanting:

From within this dirt small seeds do be,
Way to small for thee to see,
Yet from the life force in the seeds,
Hair shall grow like nasty weeds.

Once you have a thick mixture, stop and use the cloth to strain the muddy water. It is this muddy water which contains the hair growing magic. This water should then be mixed with shampoo and applied to your head to help your hair grow.

Diet Spells

Diet spells are spells dealing with your body. Although diet spells should never replace proper nutrition and exercise they can be used to as a means to an end. Whether using these spells to help you gain weight or lose weight, these spells can assist you in achieving your goal.

Diet Spells #1 – Gain Weight

Items needed to perform this spell: 1 small black candle. Matches. Rock Salt. 1 silver spoon. 1 tablespoon of vinegar. 1 cup of water. 1 non plastic cup.

Light the candle and heat the cup. Add the vinegar and some of rock salt, allowing the rock salt to dissolve completely in the vinegar. Boil the vinegar away. While the vinegar is being   boiled say the following chant:

Witch's brew and devil's lot,
Boil the liquid in this cup.
From the flame from down below,
Darkness enters; the crystals grow.

When the vinegar is boiled away, add the water to the cup and stir with the spoon. Chant the following until the water boils:

Crystals with the water mix,
In this cup and magic bliss;
Make a potion to make them grow;
They who drink this potion know.

When the water comes to a boil you can blow out the candle and let the potion cool. Drink the potion to begin your weight gain journey.

Diet Spells #2 – Lose Weight

Items needed to perform this spell: A dash of cinnamon. 1 crystal cup or glass. A dash of salt. 1 teaspoon of vinegar. ½ cup of water.

Mix the water and vinegar together in the crystal cup or glass. While mixing the ingredients say the following:

Add to this class from which I'll drink
The vile taste one's surely think.

The throw in a dash of salt saying:

And a bit of salt to kill the taste
Of my life I shall not waste

Then toss in a dash of cinnamon saying:

And finally a touch of spice
To make my body slim and nice

Swirl the entire mixture around with the cup in both hands. Hold it above your head and say:

With this potion that I drink
I'll lose the weight that I think
I need to lose and then some more
This magic potion born of war.

Then drink the entire potion.

Diet Spells #3 – Mirror Weight Loss Spell

Items needed to perform this spell: 1 pink candle. Oil of your choosing. 1 brown candle

This spell should be performed during the waning moon. Anoint the pink candle with the oil of your choosing. Light the pink candle. Engrave the number of pounds you desire to lose in the brown candle. Light the brown candle. Visualize banishing the excess weight.

Diet Spells #4 – Muscle Gaining Spell

Items needed to perform this spell: 1 red candle. 1 white candle. 1 picture of what you wish to look like. Fire. Cauldron to contain the fire

Place the white candle on your right and the red candle on your left. Light the candles. Hold the picture tightly, against your body and close your eyes. Light a fire in the cauldron. Say the following:

To look like this is my wish
Make my body change
For I am not happy with who I may be

Burn the picture in the fire and repeat the chant again while the picture is burning.

Diet Spells #5 – Spell to Lose Weight Faster

Items needed to perform this spell: 1 White Candle. Piece of paper. Plate.

Find a quiet location to perform this spell. On the piece of paper write how much weight you would like to lose. Light the white candle. Burn the paper while saying the following:

Burn, Burn, Burn Away
Burn these stubborn pounds away.

Put the burning piece of paper on the plate ensuring the paper burns all the way through.
Perform this spell every day for one week.

Energy Spells

Energy spells allow the spell-caster to create fields of energy around their person or someone of your own choosing. This field of energy is used to help protect you against evil magic while also aiding in good magic spells cast upon you.

Energy Spells #1 – Energy Ball Spell
Items needed to perform this spell: None

Sit in a comfortable position and begin meditating. Cup your hands together and visualize energy dots hovering all around your palms. Visualize these energy dots gathering together and forming a ball of energy.

It may take several attempts to achieve the forming of the energy ball. Do not give up, simply remain focused and repeat the ritual until you have achieved the formation of the energy ball.

Energy Spells #2 – Energy Leech Spell
Items needed to perform this spell: None

Find an object to draw upon its energy. This can be the sun, moon, or earth. Imagine energy in the form of either a ball or a beam of light coming towards you and flowing in through your head or through the palm of your hands. After a few minutes, you will feel recharged.

Energy Spells #3 – Spell to Get a New Power
Items needed to perform this spell: 1 yellow candle. Frankincense

At your alter, light the yellow candle followed by lighting the frankincense. After they are both lit, sit in a relaxing position and close your eyes. Picture an orb of universal energy swarming around your person and mixing with your aura. Visualize this energy absorbing into you, while feeling it course throughout your body. When you begin to feel empowered say the following:

In this night from which you have come,
Give me a gift not two just one.
Help to see within and without,
With this new found energy power come without a doubt.
As I do will, so shall it be.

Energy Spells #4 – Absorbing Magical Energy
Items needed to perform this spell: An Object.

Locate a large object to focus and draw upon. Place your power hand on the object. Visualize yourself extracting the energy from this object. While holding onto the object and visualizing close your eyes and say the following.

I am drained, I am drained
Return my magic unto me.
Oh mighty God, hear my plea,
I am drained, I am drained.

You can perform this spell as often and for as long as you like. The longer you perform this spell the more energy you will be able to extract. Do not perform this spell on another individual.

Energy Spells #5 – Refuel your Energy Spell
Items needed to perform this spell: Music. Rose Quartz. Vervain

This spell should be performed when alone. Light the Varvain and place the rose quartz next to it. Turn on your music. Dance to the music.

Dream Spells

Dream spells are spells that can be used for a variety of reasons. Reasons such as help with interpreting your dreams, protection from nightmares, implanting dreams into your mind and so on.

Dream Spells #1 – Getting Answers from a Dream
Items needed to perform this spell: A yellow piece of paper. Dried rose petals. Calendula flowers. Poppy box.

Take a dry box of poppy and purge it from the seeds. Write your answer on a yellow piece of paper, and then place it in the poppy box. Boil the roses. Before bedtime, place the Calendula flowers under your pillow and the poppy box on your bed. Drink the boiled rose soup. Think about your problems, think about your options. The answer to your question will come in your dream.

Dream Spells #2 – Calm Dream Spell
Items needed to perform this spell: None

Before lying down for bed, relax and slowly chant the following 5 times. Say the chant slower each time.

Earth, Wind, Fire, and Air Forth you are called Dim the stars Brighten my dreams with hope.

Dream Spells #3 – Dream Protection Spell
Items needed to perform this spell: 1 tablespoon of lemon juice. 1 tablespoon of sea salt.
1 teaspoon of vegetable oil. 1 cauldron. 1 piece of paper. 2 black candles. 1 pen

Mix the sea salt, oil and lemon juice in the cauldron. Place the cauldron in front of you on the floor. Place the candles beside the cauldron, one on the left and one on the right of you. Tear the piece of paper in half and place it aside. Light both candles. Close your eyes and visualize a sphere. Visualize yourself stuck inside the middle of the sphere, trying to get out. With your eyes still closes, visualize the candles burning around you. Watch the candle flames spinning around you, spinning faster and faster. Visualize yourself being released from the sphere. Open your eyes. On one piece of the torn paper, draw a picture of what you saw. On the other, write down your biggest fear. Light both pieces of paper on fire, using the candle fire. Throw each piece of paper into the cauldron. Take the cauldron and pour its contents into a hole in the ground. Cover the hole with dirt. The spell is now complete and your dreams will be protected.

Dream Spells #4 – Create Your Own Nightmares Spell
Items needed to perform this spell: white scarf. 4 cloves. Pinch of basil. Pinch of ground sage. Vanilla oil. Black marker. White ribbon.

Lay the scarf out in a straight pattern. Place the spices into the scarf and add 2 drops of oil. Gather the scarf and and tie it with the ribbon. On the outside of the scarf draw the nightmare that plagues you. Place the scarf under your pillow and sleep with it there

Dream Spells #5 – Control Your Dreams Spell
Items needed to perform this spell: A small box with a lid.

Each night before you go to bed, open your box and hold your hand over it and say the following.

May this Dream Box enhance my dreams while I sleep. May the visions be clear and may I hold them so deep. So mote it be

Place your box as close to your bed as possible. If you want to dream about something specific, simply ask for it.

Dream Spells #6 – Sweet Dreams Spell
Items needed to perform this spell: Nothing

Place one hand on your chest. Imagine floating on a cloud falling into a deep sleep. Say the following chant:

*Dreams be sweet tonight
As I lay here,
Nightmares be cast away*

Into the night,
Don't show your face
Dreams be sweet tonight.

When you fall asleep you will have sweet dreams.

Dream Spells #7 – Realistic Dream Spell
Items needed to perform this spell: None

Relax and focus on your inner peace. Say the following chant before going to bed.

I like my thoughts and I like my dreams, so let me make my feel real.

Dream Spells #8 – Dream Recall Spell
Items needed to perform this spell: 1 cup chamomile tea. Dried crushed Lavender. 1 white handkerchief.

Place the lavender inside the handkerchief. Fold neatly. Place the handkerchief between your pillow and pillowcase. Drink the tea. Recite the following incantation three times:

From my higher self I bid thee come from the deep rushing river of my dreams -- great winged thoughts of inspiration, knowledge, growth, and learning. I welcome with joy the symbols and vivid colors brought forth, up through the depths of my mind, and I will remember only those dreams that are significant. I will decode these with little difficulty upon waking by using the keyword (insert a special word of choice here). So mote it be.

Close your eyes and go to sleep. This spell may not work right away; it could take up to several weeks before you are able to recall significant parts of your dream segments.

Protection Spells

Protection spells deal with power and force spells. These spells create a shield or barrier around you that will prohibit evil magic from harming you.

Protection Spells #1 – A Spell of Protection
Items needed to perform this spell: 1 Candle.

Sit before your candle. Light the candle. Look into the flame. Visualize fire bathing you with glowing protective light. The fire creates a flaming, shimmering sphere around you as you say the following:

Craft the spell
In the fire
Craft it well
Weave it higher
Weave it now
Of simmering flame
None shall come
To hurt or maim
None shall pass
This fiery wall
None shall pass
No, none at all

Repeat as often as needed.

Protection Spells #2 – A Child's Protection Sachet

Items needed to perform this spell: White handkerchief. Several strands of loose dog hair. Two strands of your own hair. Picture of your child. Any protection herb. Black yarn or thread.

Place the picture of your child on the cloth along with your hair, the dog hair and a sprinkle of the protection herb. Bring together the corners of the cloth and tie it with the black yarn or thread, while focusing on protecting your child. When done, you can place the Sachet in your child's room, in your room, or give to your child to carry.

Protection Spells #3 – Protect You and Your Loved Ones from Harm

Items needed to perform this spell: 2/4's Cup of Spring Water. 1 Teaspoon Vervain.
2 Tablespoons Sea Salt. 2 Tablespoons each of Frankincense and Myrrh. Cauldron or bowl.

Mix all of the ingredients in a cauldron or bowl. Sprinkle the spring water very lightly around your home in discreet places and anoint the bottom of your shoes and those of loved ones. Immediately dispose of any leftover potion.

Protection Spells #4 – Protection of the Moon

Items needed to perform this spell: None

This spell is best performed during a full moon. Say the following chant:

On this very night I call upon the protection of the moon
I ask you to protect me and let my health be in full bloom
Protect me and my family, this I ask
I ask you humbly to do this very task

Protection Spells #5 – Protection Chant to Ease Your Mind of Worries

Items needed to perform this spell: None

Say the following chant:
Elements of the Sun,
Elements of the Day,
Come this way,

Powers of night and day,
I summon thee,
I call upon thee,
To Protect me,
So Shall it Be.

Protection Spells #6 – Protection from Anger Spell
Items needed to perform this spell: 7 White Candles. A needle. A cork. A bowl of spring water. Tongs.

Place the cork in the bowl of spring water. Place the seven candles in a circle and as you light each one, repeat the following:

Burn you now with the heat of anger

When all of the candles have been lighted, hold the needle with the tongs and place the tip of the needle into each of the candle flames. As you place the tip of the needle in each flame, repeat the following:

Draw the anger, pierce the flame, draw the anger, pierce the flame, draw the anger, and pierce the flame.

When you have repeated this process with each candle, drop the needle into the bowl of water with the cork. Extinguish the candles.

Take the needle and push it into the cork. As you do, say the following:

Anger, I confine you! With this spell I imprison you by the cleansing spirit of the water and by the authority of that spirit plead the air does stop your flight.

Take the bowl of water and sprinkle it lightly around your bed. Then place the cork, with the needle in it somewhere in the room in which you sleep.

Protection Spells #7 – Book of Shadows Stay Out of Prying Eyes Protection Spell
Items needed to perform this spell: Athame. Salt. Your Book of Shadows.

Say the following chant:

My Guardian Angels and Spirit Guides, keep my book of shadows safe from all malice and evil intentions and from prying eyes.

Then sprinkle the salt on the book.

Protection Spells #8 – Circle of Protection Spell
Items needed to perform this spell: None

This spell should be performed in an area in which you would like protected, such as your home or place of work. Say the following chant:

In this circle that is home,
No evil shall be free to roam.
All this evil now will cease,
I vanquish you with words of peace.

Protection Spells #9 – Deflect Dark Magic Spell
Items needed to perform this spell: None

Say the following chant with authority in your voice:

Power of objection, magic of deflection. Assist me in this task be done, banish this darkness with the power of the sun.

Protection Spells #10 – Elemental Protection Spell
Items needed to perform this spell: None.

Focus your thoughts and energies on remaining safe and calm. Do this for several minutes. When you feel connected with your energy and your mind, cast the circle and say the following:

Terra, Ignis, Aqua
All Three
Elements of astral, I summon thee
Earth by divinity, divinity by earth
Give thy enemy the power to see
The strength of the elements by my side
Rules of magic, I shall abide
Now, when my enemy meets his/her/its downfall
This spell will have no power left at all

In no way will this spell reverse
Or place upon me any curse
As Above--So Below, Blessed Be!

Binding Spells

Binding spells are used to hold or bind things. One of the main reasons to perform binding spells is to bind a spirit, person or entity person from doing damage to yourself or your loved ones. You can also perform binding spells on an individual to prevent them from harming themselves.

Binding Spells #1 – Simple Binding Spell

Items needed to perform this spell: Paper. Black Pen. A Rubber Band.

On a 3 x 3 piece of paper, write the name of the person that is to be bound using the black ink pen. As you write the name of this person, visualize his or her face. When you have written the name cross it with an inverted pentagram.

Fold the paper twice, tying it with the rubber band. Raise the tied paper to your temple and chant the following 3 times:

To be protected from you,
This magic charm I will do,
With these words I bind thee,
For you to let me be,
To be protected from your harm,
I now seal this charm

Place the paper under your right shoe and slam your foot on the ground nine times. As you slam it the ninth time say...

So Mote it Be.

Binding Spells #2 – Spell to Bind a Person
Items needed to perform this spell: An object that belongs to this person or a picture of this person. Tape.

Take the object or picture of this person and bind it with tape while saying the following 3 times:

(Person's name) I bind you from doing harm to others or yourself.

Binding Spells #3 – Binding with Fear from Harming You Spell
Items needed to perform this spell: A picture of the person you wish to bind. Black thread.

Take the picture of the person you wish to bind with fear and tie it with the black string or thread, after that hang it in a place where it won't be found and will be in the dark as you hang it say the following :

This is the image of my would be victim
Hang it from a single thread
In a place no one shall see
It will bring fear in the heart of him
Who shall harm me
He will be binded by fear from harming me further
He will be binded by fear from harming me at all
I will tie a knot in the thread when I wish
To secure the fear until I break it
So mote it be.

Binding Spells #4 – Binding Your Anger Spell
Items needed to perform this spell: Dirt or Sand

Hold some dirt or sand in your right hand. Poor your anger into the dirt or sand and say the following:

Anger I bind within my hand,
Now I toss it to the land

With harm to none,
And for the good of all, so shall it be!

Throw the sand or dirt over your shoulder and walk
away. Do not look back.

Binding Spells #5 – White Magic Binding Spell

Items needed to perform this spell: Picture of person you wish to bind. 1 Sealable
bag. Water with salt mixed into it.

On the back of the picture write the name of the person you wish to bind. Also
write what you would like for this person to stop doing to you. Place the picture in
a sealable bag then pour in the salt water and say the following:

Bound in ice
You are my vice
Frozen forever
Unbinding never

I cast this spell
No more lies you shall tell
With my power and might
I bind you (name of person) this very night

Seal the bag and place it in your freezer.

In Closing

 When done correctly spell-casting has the potential to produce very powerful changes within your life, positive changes. With the proper focus and dedication to the craft you will begin to notice a peace around you that you have never felt before.

Just remember, magic is a powerful tool and should never be taken for granted.

~Blessed Be! ~

Roc Marten

APPENDIX I

The Wiccan Rede

Bide the Wiccan Laws we must, in Perfect Love and Perfect Trust

Soft of eye and light of touch, we speak little and listen much

We heed flower, bush, and tree, by the Lady blessed be

Revere all life; respect all things, to us great blessings the Forces bring

When we have a true need, we hearken not to other's greed

With no fool a season spend, lest we be counted as his or her friend

Merry we meet and merry we part, bright our cheeks and warm our heart

With everything we live and let live, we fairly take and we fairly give

We wear the pentacle to remind us of, The Lady and Lord and their Divine Love

We cast the circle thrice about, to keep unwanted energies out

To bind the spell every time, every spell we speak in rhyme

Greater Power will this lend, and to our will all things do bend

In our hands the Power we hold, to make the new and recreate the old

And whether or not we win or lose, we always respect others' right to choose

We work for the Good of everyone, the spell is cast and it is done

Both Lady and Lord so Divine, You show us a way and give us a sign

The four tools of the Lady and Lord, Cup, Wand, Pentacle, and Sword

Where the rippling waters go, we cast a stone and truth we know

When in doubt the cards make clear, all that we have need to hear

Divination always shows the way, truth is shown come what may

It's not what we do but what we intend, that determines how all things will end

Harm comes from thought as well as deed, every thought we think is a seed

Each time it's repeated the power flows, into the seed and stronger it grows

The power is always amply supplied, for all that we do is multiplied

Mind the Threefold Law we should, three times bad and three times good

This warning we must always heed, when following the Wiccan Rede

All things in time as the Wheel turns round, to the cycles of life we are bound

Cross quarters and quarters we do keep great blessings all year round we reap

Respect the phases of the Moon, with the cycles of life we live in tune

Blessed by day and blessed by night, guided always by the Light

Of Infinite Love in everything, with hearts uplifted and souls that sing

We know our work is truly done, when we wish Peace and Love to everyone

The Wiccan Rede we do fulfill: "An ye harm none, do as ye will."

More Wiccan Books from PDP Publications

Wiccan Chants

The Modern Day Spellbook

The Wiccan Guide to Candle Magic

Witches in the Kitchen: Recipes for the Eight Sabbats

ARADIA, or the Gospel of the Witches

PDP Publications

Revised Edition
First Printing 2012
Cover Art by M. Cage

Made in the USA
Middletown, DE
10 November 2015